Making A Difference

4

MAKING A DIFFERENCE

"The least of you will become a thousand, the smallest a mighty nation. I am the LORD; in its time I will do this swiftly"

ISAIAH 60:22

Operation Timothy

OT

CBMC Publications

The Christian Business Men's Committee is an international evangelical organization of Christian business and professional men whose primary purpose is to present Jesus Christ as Savior and Lord to other business and professional men and to train these men to carry out the Great Commission.

CBMC of USA is a nondenominational, non-profit Christian ministry supported by gifts from people committed to reaching and discipling business and professional men for Jesus Christ.

More information may be obtained by writing:
Christian Business Men's Committee of USA
1800 McCallie Avenue
Chattanooga, Tennessee 37404
1-800-575-2262

Operation Timothy is an investigative Bible study with the goal of helping people to grow spiritually. It has been designed to serve as a link with the Living Proof I and II Video Series.
For more information, call 1-800-575-2262

Rob Suggs, *writer, cartoonist*

Isa Williams, *graphic designer*

Operation Timothy Workbook 4 – ISBN # 0-945292-05-8

Contents

APPOINTMENTS

Next Meeting _____ **Time** _____
_____
_____
_____
_____

Next Meeting _____ **Time** _____
_____
_____
_____
_____

Next Meeting _____ **Time** _____
_____
_____
_____
_____

Next Meeting _____ **Time** _____
_____
_____
_____
_____

Next Meeting _____ **Time** _____
_____
_____
_____

Next Meeting _____ **Time** _____
_____
_____
_____

CHAPTER ONE

1 Bringing It Home

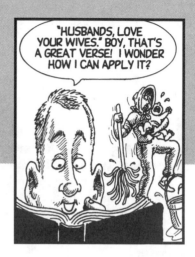

That's What They Say:

Success in marriage consists not only in finding the right mate, but also in being the right mate. ANONYMOUS

The most important thing a father can do for his children is to love their mother. THEODORE HESBURGH

Troubles in marriage often start when a man is so busy earning his salt that he forgets his sugar. ANONYMOUS

Changing Times. This is one impatient caterpillar. He looks in the mirror and isn't pleased with the image. Efforts to fly have brought disastrous results. When does the butterfly part begin? New Christians often feel the same way. We make the common error of forcing change from the outside in. But like the butterfly's cocoon, spiritual change begins on the inside — with the very manner in which we view reality. As God's worldview takes root, ultimately values and behavior will be transformed. This is imperative as we integrate our faith into our family situations.

Living Proof II Video Series provides a vivid illustration of this process through drama.

In your view, what past or present television show best describes the current status of the American family:

a. Home Improvement
b. The Brady Bunch
c. All in the Family
d. Cosby
e. Married With Children
f. Other: _____

Which of the selections best describes your family? Why? _____

_____

_____

_____

THE BIG PICTURE.

In this chapter we'll examine one of the most important arenas of change: the family.

This chapter is designed to include everyone — married or single. These principles on relationships can be adapted and applied to marriage, parents, children, and friendships. As you work through this lesson, first identify the primary application, then apply that principle in your own relationships.

I. Relationships
II. Reality
III. Reflections

I. RELATIONSHIPS

Building Blocks. The house isn't built overnight; but as we follow the blueprint there are guidelines for solid construction. Ephesians 4 and 5 provide a lifestyle strategy Christians can follow from the beginning.

Ephesians 4:25–5:21. Using the following chart, review the positive and negative guidelines for all of our relationships.

Positive	Negative
speak the truth in love	stop lying
be angry	don't sin in your anger or let sun go down on anger or give devil foothold in anger
work in order to share	stop stealing
build others up with words	don't speak unwholesome words don't grieve the Holy Spirit
be kind, compassionate forgive each other as God forgave you	get rid of all bitterness, rage, anger, brawling, slander, malice
be imitators of God, live a life of love	don't even hint at sexual immorality, impurity, or greed no obscenity, foolish talk, coarse joking don't be partners with those who do these things
live as children of light find out what pleases God	don't have anything to do with unfruitful deeds of darkness, expose them instead
be careful how you live, live as wise people, be filled with Spirit, sing, make music to Lord, always give thanks to God, submit to one another	don't live as unwise people don't get drunk

Which one of these most needs your attention? What will you do to work on this?

_____

_____

Marriage Principles. In Genesis 2:18, God not only created Adam, but for the first time in His creation, He made the statement that something was not good. That "something" was the fact that Adam was alone. Even though Adam had fellowship with God Himself, and this was before the Fall, God said it was not good that Adam was alone. Therefore, God created Eve in order to remove Adam's aloneness as well as to meet and complete Adam. But, how does this happen? Are marriages today reflecting the fulfillment of these purposes? If not, why not? Let's look at the operating principles God has given for a healthy, wholesome marriage. There are many, but we will look at five of them:

1. Love your wife
2. Respect your husband
3. Humble yourself
4. Understand differences/meet needs
5. Keep "fanning the flame"

We will study Ephesians 5:21-33 to discover God's blueprint for the husband/wife relationship.

1. Love your wife

In Ephesians 5:25-29, what three things did Christ do for the church?

_____

_____

What do you think it means for a husband to "give himself up" for his wife in the same way that Christ did for the church? What would that look like in your relationship with your wife?

_____

_____

What does it mean to "feed and care for" your wife (King James version says "nourish and cherish")? How can you do this?

_____

_____

What will it cost you?

_____

_____

Ephesians 5:32 says that marriage is a _____ _____ .

To what other relationship does God compare the husband and wife relationship in verse 32? How does this affect your view of marriage and the family? _____

_____

2. Respect your husband

There are two aspects to this matter of respect that the Bible refers to as reverence and submission. These are often misunderstood and abused terms. God gives a balanced view of each person's responsibilities. People often distort God's clear teaching on these areas.

In Ephesians 5:33 what does it mean for a wife to respect her husband?

_____

_____

Why do you think God tells the wife to respect, rather than love, her husband?

_____

_____

What is the wife instructed to do in verse 22? Who is the wife's model in this principle?

_____

_____

"Submission" is a negative word in our culture today. Why do you think this is so?

_____

_____

How do you understand verse 22 in light of verses 21, 25 and 29?

_____

_____

What has your experience been with this principle of respect and submission?

_____

_____

3. Humble yourself

Compare Ephesians 5:21 and 1 Peter 5:5-6. What is the relationship between humility and submission?

_____

_____

_____

According to verse 6, what is God's attitude toward the proud? Toward the humble?

_____

_____

Grade yourself on humility:
    a. Hard to be humble when you're as perfect as me.
    b. I'm humble — and very proud of it!
    c. I know my place.
    d. Under "modest," the dictionary has my picture.
    e. I find it difficult to say I am wrong.
    f. Other _____

> Those who travel the high road of humility are not troubled by heavy traffic.
>
> SENATOR ALAN K. SIMPSON

How can your humility make a difference?

_____

_____

_____

Review Living Proof II, Session 7 or read chapter 8, Lifestyle Discipleship, Jim Petersen.

Review chart on page 39 in Operation Timothy Book III, Living With Power.

4. Understand differences/meet needs

Many books have been written on the differences between men and women, but we still tend to view our spouses from our own perspective. Understanding the crucial differences between men and women, and the specific differences between you and your spouse are essential areas to explore and discover.

What are some of the differences that you have discovered between you and your spouse? _____

_____

What will you do to discover and understand these differences in a deeper way?

_____

_____

I Peter 3:7 instructs the husband to be considerate and treat his wife with respect for what reason? _____

Does this mean the wife is inferior or superior? Explain.

_____

_____

_____

Assessing the unique priority of needs in individuals

Although we all have the same basic needs, the priority of these needs may differ with each individual. A husband's greatest need may be respect, while his wife's greatest need may be attention. One child may particularly need affection, while another may be especially blessed by approval. If we're not careful, we'll not only treat everyone the same (as if they all had the same priority of needs), but we'll go about meeting other people's needs based on what our priority of needs are. An important aspect of learning to love an individual is taking the time to know them and to discover what their unique needs are.

Write down the name of your spouse, children, close relatives, and best friends and list (in order of priority) what you think their 3 most important needs are. Then ask them for their opinion. Consider these needs: acceptance, approval, encouragement, support, affection, security, respect, attention, comfort, appreciation.

Need	Definition	Scripture
ACCEPTANCE	Deliberate and ready reception with favorable positive response.	ROMANS 15:7
AFFECTION	To communicate care and closeness through physical touch.	ROMANS 16:16
APPRECIATION (PRAISE)	To communicate with words and feeling personal gratefulness for another.	I CORINTHIANS 11:2
APPROVAL	Expressed commendation; to think and speak well of.	ROMANS 14:18
ATTENTION (CARE)	To take thought of another and convey appropriate interest, support, etc.; to enter into another's "world."	I CORINTHIANS 12:25
COMFORT (EMPATHY)	To come alongside with word, feeling and touch; to give consolation with tenderness.	I THESSALONIANS 4:18
ENCOURAGEMENT	To urge forward and positively persuade toward a goal.	I THES. 5:11, HEB. 10:24
RESPECT (HONOR)	To value and regard highly; to convey great worth.	ROMANS 12:10
SECURITY (PEACE)	Confidence of "harmony" in relationship; free from harm.	MARK 9:50
SUPPORT	Come alongside and gently help carry a load (problem, struggle).	GALATIANS 6:2

Center For Marriage and Family Intimacy, David Ferguson

Spouse (Name) _____

   My opinion _____

   Their opinion _____

Child (Name) _____

   My opinion _____

   Their opinion _____

Relative (Name) _____

   My opinion _____

   Their opinion _____

Friend (Name) _____

   My opinion _____

   Their opinion _____

Now write down your top 3 needs.

_____   _____   _____

Ask your spouse or friend to write down what he/she thinks your top 3 needs are.

_____   _____   _____

How could you begin to meet one of the needs of your loved one? _____

_____

_____

Did you learn anything new or were there any surprises? _____

_____

_____

This exercise is taken from the book, *Top Ten Intimacy Needs*, by Dr. David Ferguson and Dr. Don McMinn (and used by their permission).

5. Keep "fanning the flame"

Is the flame in your marriage glowing brightly or almost flickering out? How do you keep "fanning the flame" and keep the romance alive in your relationship? How do you keep growing in intimacy in your other relationships — children, parents, siblings?

Your best ability: availability. It has been said that in families, love is spelled T-I-M-E. Keeping in mind that marriage is compared to the relationship between Christ and the church, how does this principle challenge you about the time you spend with your spouse, children, and other family members?

Drs. Minirth and Meier, authors of *"Happiness is a Choice,"* recommend the following in the pursuit of "bringing it home."

> *Spend a little time nearly every day getting more intimate with your mate and children. Parents, brothers, sisters, and other close relatives should also have a high priority. Do all you can to resolve family conflicts...Intimacy with your family is more vital to your self-worth and overall mental health than most people imagine...We both spend an average of two hours each weeknight and four hours each Saturday and Sunday playing with our children. The old saying, "It's not the quantity but the quality of time spent with your children that's important," is nonsense! The quantity of time is just as important as the quality of time. We also take time every day to communicate with our wives on a deep and intimate level. We also take our wives out on dates at least once a week. And we are frequently thinking of things that will cultivate intimate friendships with our parents, brothers, sisters, and other close relatives...We must take the initiative ourselves in resolving old family conflicts.*

Drs. Minirth and Meier are two very busy doctors, and yet they set aside priority time to play with their children and spend sharing times with their wives and other family members. Spend some time reflecting on your week and daily schedule. How much time each week are you currently spending with your spouse? Children? Other family members? _____

_____

Perhaps you need to pencil in time with your children and spouse for each day in your notebook/planner just like you do your business and other appointments.

How do you think your spouse/children would respond to receiving this kind of attention and priority from you? _____

_____

Use the following chart as a worksheet for the next few weeks: (Note times and possible activities with each family member. It doesn't have to be expensive; playing a board game, or asking questions and listening intently, or taking a walk — there are many options — the focus is on getting to know the other person and letting them get to know you as you really are.)

	Monday	Tuesday	Wednesday	Thursday	Friday	Saturday	Sunday
7 am							
8 am							
9 am							
10 am							
11 am							
12 am							
1 pm							
2 pm							
3 pm							
4 pm							
5 pm							
6 pm							
7 pm							
8 pm							
9 pm							
10 pm							

Have your spouse (child, parent, sibling) tell you three things that you could do that would please her/him (often this involves stopping something that is irritating or doing something that has been neglected — so be prepared!)

II. REALITY

No one goes into marriage planning to make a mess out of it. However, that is often the result. How does this happen? There are volumes written on this subject, and the answer is complex. We will look at three of four major areas that seem to be the most common, knotty problem-areas in marriage and the home. The fourth area, "Handling Money" will be covered in depth in Chapter 3.

1. Resolving conflict
2. Developing and protecting sexual intimacy
3. Dealing with spiritual differences
4. Handling money

1. Resolving conflict

Family Feud. According to Proverbs 13:10 (NIV), _____ only breeds

quarrels, but _____ is found in those who_____

_____.

What is a key principle in dealing with conflict in Proverbs 15:1-2?

_____

_____

Is anger or arguing necessarily bad? _____

Some people and couples seldom disagree because they are afraid of "arguing." They often sacrifice the truth about what they think and feel and learn to "stuff" their real reactions. Others vent their anger at every opportunity, blowing off steam like a volcano, and injuring the other in the process. Ephesians 4:25-32 gives some needed balance to this issue. Read this passage and answer the following questions:

What does it mean "In your anger do not sin: do not let the sun go down while you are still angry..." _____

_____

_____

What does it mean to "put off falsehood and speak truthfully" or in another translation "to speak the truth in love?" _____

_____

_____

Do you "love" people to the exclusion of speaking the truth to them, especially if the truth is unpleasant or painful? Or are you one of those who speaks the truth, but does it bluntly and unlovingly? _____

_____

Which would your spouse (family or friends) say is your most frequent way of dealing with conflict and other issues? _____

_____

_____

Spend some time asking God to help you gain more balance in this area of handling your anger, speaking the truth and loving others. If you are a "stuffer," ask Him to give you the courage to speak the truth even though it is painful to do so. If you are a "blower," ask Him to give you self-control and more loving ways to express the truth, and wisdom when to keep quiet.

> **The book of Proverbs has much to say about the use of our tongue.**

What encouraging related fact is found in 1 Corinthians 10:13?

_____

_____

_____

Handling anger is one of the toughest areas for human beings to learn. Depression can often be traced to turning our anger in upon ourselves.

> *Do all you can to resolve family conflicts. Don't ever get vengeance on family members. Heal the wounds as best you can and leave the rest up to God... Unresolved family conflicts can continue for years and years...We must take the initiative ourselves in resolving old family conflicts. We must not keep at a distance until out relatives "repent" for hurting our feelings. The most mature thing we can do is to assume 100% of the responsibility for resolving family conflicts, then pray that we can discover creative ways in which to achieve reconciliation. If these efforts fail, we must try new measures.* MINIRTH, MEIER HAPPINESS IS A CHOICE

List one or more unresolved family hurts/conflicts with which you are struggling from the past or present. _____

_____

_____

_____

What is one thing you can do this week to take the initiative in resolving one conflict?

_____

_____

2. Developing and protecting sexual intimacy

What are the principles regarding sexual intimacy in marriage in I Corinthians 7:2-5?

_____

_____

Why are these principles so important according to verse 5? _____

_____

_____

What does Hebrews 13:4 reveal about God's heart toward this area of marriage?

_____

_____

Compare Ephesians 5:3 with Proverbs 6:24-29. How do these relate with the world's current standards for sexuality? _____

_____

_____

Why do you feel this particular standard is important to God? _____

_____

_____

What do you think these verses imply about God's priority for marriage? Explain.

_____

_____

_____

From your own observation, how does adultery affect children? _____

_____

_____

_____

Read the following letter written by a 6th grade girl, age 12.

MY TEDDY BEAR IS LONELY

There once was a little boy who took his teddy bear with him everywhere he went. One evening when his mother called him in for bed, he left his teddy bear leaning against a tree where he had been playing. The next day the little teddy bear waited all day for his friend. The boy seemed to have forgotten all about him. Day after day passed, and the boy never came back for his little friend.

This was the story that went on in my head as I drew a picture of a sad teddy bear leaning against a tree after I was told my parents were getting a divorce. My dad was leaving us, and I wanted to draw him a picture to show him how I felt. I was only eight years old then, and I didn't know how to put my feelings into words. At the top of my teddy bear picture I wrote "I'm lonely."

Looking back, I know I was trying to say that I felt all alone. Now that I am almost twelve, I can put my feelings into words much better. Over the past four years, I have had many different feelings about my parent's divorce. I am sad that I don't have a father anymore. He says we still have him, but he is in another state, so it doesn't count. He's not here when we need him. He is not here to love us and pay attention to us.

I am angry that Daddy moved away and left us to be with his new girl-friend. I feel betrayed that he married her, because he already had a wife and children of his own. He just left me like I was nobody.

Mommy and Daddy get me all confused, because they both tell me two different stories. I feel like I am in the middle, and I have to choose sides.

The money problem is the worst. It's not fair that Daddy buys things for his new wife and her girls, and when we visit, he says he doesn't have any money to buy us anything. It is very hard for us to live because Mommy doesn't make much money, and Daddy isn't good about sending the child support. I'm tired of us not having money for the things we need.

Today, Daddy called me on the phone. I finally told him my teddy bear story. He said he understood that I was saying that he was the boy and me the teddy bear. He talked for a while. I didn't say much. I think he half understood what I feel and half not. He said he hopes I don't feel like he doesn't love me anymore. He says he still loves me. The only thing that counts is that we are friends and keep in touch all the time. He says talking to me is one of the most important things in his life.

I feel like crying a lot because I have lots of feelings blocked up inside me, and some days it just all comes pouring out because of holding it in. Someday I hope I'll feel better about my parent's divorce. But for now it hurts too much to think it will ever be better.

Britain Culpepper, Grade 6

What are your reactions as you read this? _____

_____

_____

_____

_____

Were you affected in this way as a child? Explain. _____

_____

_____

Have you been in the parent's position in this story? Explain. _____

_____

_____

_____

_____

What do you do with the hurt and pain of these experiences? Read I John 1:9 and James 5:16. How could these verses bring healing into your life? _____

_____

_____

_____

3. Dealing with spiritual differences

You are a brand-new Christian, excited about your faith and your new-found joy and peace. You can't wait to share Christ with your spouse, children, parents, friends. However, when you do, you find them less than enthusiastic; in fact, they often are resistant, antagonistic, and mocking toward you. Has this been your experience? Explain.

_____

_____

_____

_____

The Bible gives several key principles in dealing with these issues.

What are Paul's instructions to young Timothy in 2 Timothy 2:23-26 on the attitudes and behavior that should characterize us? _____

_____

_____

List the attitudes in Philippians 2:1-5 which should guide us.

_____

_____

_____

I Peter 3:1-9 gives principles to both the wife and husband. Outline these principles and explain their importance in your life. _____

_____

_____

_____

_____

_____

_____

_____

_____

Key: Don't focus on changing others; focus on the changes you need to make to become more like Christ.

Many new Christians who try to bring their new-found faith home to their family members encounter a lot of resistance and sometimes resentment. Often, these family members are looking to see the changes in your life and attitudes before they are willing to listen to your words. Try working on the areas suggested in this lesson, such as loving them, getting to know their needs and meeting them, spending more time with them and resolving old family conflicts. Then, ask God for the wisdom to know when they are ready to "hear" the words that have made such a difference in your life.

III. REFLECTIONS

Making it practical:

(These suggestions are geared towards a spouse, but if you are unmarried adapt these suggestions for your children, parents, sister/brother, or a friend.)

Discuss the answers from this lesson during special times of sharing such as:
- Marriage "staff" meetings — a designated time each week when husband and wife can vulnerably share issues of the heart.
- Family nights — special times of sharing which may include a family meal and fun activities.
- Enrichment groups/classes — for couples, singles, or families.

1. Consider sending your spouse a card or flowers once a week for several weeks.

2. Make a decision before God
   a) not to criticize your spouse publicly, and
   b) to praise your spouse publicly and privately.

3. How much time do you spend talking with your spouse on a daily basis?
   Is 20 minutes a day too much?

   Husband: _____ Wife: _____

4. Practice admiring and verbalizing to your spouse at least one positive character quality every day. Use the following list as a starter:

creative	thoughtful	steady	graceful
dependable	strong	humorous	affectionate
resourceful	gentle	lighthearted	spiritual
thorough	warm	playful	responsive
considerate	tender	carefree	trustworthy
steadfast	helpful	willing	honest
amiable	imaginative	sensual	versatile
sensitive	cheerful	romantic	friendly
caring	reliable	giving	open
happy	sincere	selfless	respectful
adaptable	wise	pleasant	forgiving
loving	tolerant	tactful	lively
kind	patient	generous	

Bringing it Home. Family. Marriage. Submission. Humility. Growth. Time. Sticky subjects, indeed! God can certainly "get personal," can't He? What is the most penetrating insight you've gained from this study?

_____

_____

_____

_____

Scripture Memory Verse:

1 Marriage	NIV

EPHESIANS 5:32-33

This is a profound mystery—but I am talking about Christ and the church. However, each one of you also must love his wife as he loves himself, and the wife must respect her husband.

EPHESIANS 5:32-33

For additional help, reading, study:

CBMC Family Conferences and books, for more information call 1-800-575-2262.

Center for Marriage and Family Intimacy, David and Theresa Ferguson
Monthly newsletter, seminars, books, counselling
    P.O. Box 201808
    Austin, Texas 78720-1808
    1-800-881-8008
Pursuit of Intimacy, Dr. David Ferguson
Intimate Encounters, Ferguson, Thurman (workbook for couples)
If You Only Knew, Dr. Gary Smalley (for men)
For Better or Best, Dr. Gary Smalley (for women)

NOTES

> **REFLECTIONS**
>
> When marriages breakdown, the children are 5 times more likely to go to prison, 5 times more likely to be involved with drugs, 11 times more likely to commit teen suicide, 5 times to commit physical abuse on their own children.

2 Taking it to Work

If you don't believe in the resurrection of the dead, you should be here five minutes before quitting time. SIGN IN A SHOP

We need to stop looking at work as simply a means of earning a living and start realizing it is one of the elemental ingredients of making a life. LUCI SWINDOLL

If you are called to be a street sweeper, sweep streets even as Michelangelo painted, or Beethoven composed music, or Shakespeare wrote poetry. Sweep streets so well that all the hosts of heaven and earth will pause to say, here lived a great sweeper who did his job well. MARTIN LUTHER KING, JR.

WARMUP

"I owe, I owe... It's off to work I go." Have you seen that bumper sticker? It brings a chuckle because we identify with the sentiment. There's the house payment, or at least that home we hope to have. If it's not the lingering college loan, it's the college fund for our children. And how about retirement?

Society's message is loud and clear: Work to earn! The motive is money. But these words are not found in Scripture. In this chapter, we'll discover what God says about careers, and how we can "take Christ to work."

"Are We Having Fun Yet?" Another bumper sticker. Just how do you feel about your job? Select the response which best represents your state of work satisfaction:

a. Peak performance! Just wish they'd let me through the door before 8:30 a.m.!
b. Job well done. Forty hours of satisfaction.
c. It's a living. Pays the bills.
d. Beam me up, Scotty!
e. Other _____

THE BIG PICTURE.

I. Attitudes towards work
II. Actions as we work
III. Example of Daniel
IV. Overloaded

I. ATTITUDES TOWARD WORK

Humanity, Inc. How did this whole work idea get started? Read Genesis 2:2-3. What is the origin of work? _____

_____

Now read Genesis 1:27. How is the identity of humanity described? _____

_____

_____

Taking those two passages together, would you conclude work is good or bad? Explain.

_____

_____

What about human work? What assignment does God give Adam? Read Genesis 2:15?

_____

_____

Good work! God ordained work for us, even in the Garden when our relationship with Him was perfect. But in the process of Adam's work — tending the garden — there was rebellion (Read Genesis 3). A part of the consequences was that work would become difficult: full of fatigue and difficulty (Genesis 3:19). The tension is realizing work's "goodness" while admitting it's difficulties. What do you notice concerning work in Genesis 3:17-19? _____

_____

_____

_____

_____

_____

Bread-winners Beware. We work because God works, and because He desires us to do so. But what about "earning a living?" The Bible's words might surprise us. What is the goal of work according to John 6:27? _____

_____

To what degree should we depend upon careers, according to Philippians 4:19? Explain. _____

_____

_____

How might this affect your view of your job? _____

_____

_____

How does this make you feel? _____

_____

_____

Divine laziness? If God will supply for us, then why work — why not relax? What does 2 Thessalonians 3:10-12 have to say on the topic of work ethic?

_____

Based on the Scripture we've reviewed so far, summarize the relationship between God, man, and work. _____

_____

_____

More Reasons to Work. God has other purposes for our work. What good thing does it enable us to do, according to Ephesians 4:28? _____

_____

_____

_____

List a few people or ministries God has placed you in a position to support through your work. _____

_____

_____

The Book of Ecclesiastes frequently deals with the issue of work and its fatigue and frustration. What does 3:12, 13 say about the enjoyment of work? _____

_____

_____

No pain, no gain. Paul was a tent-maker by trade. In Acts 18:3-4, how did he regard his work? _____

_____

What are some reasons for work found in 1 Thessalonians 4:11-12?

_____

_____

How might the spiritual principle found in James 1:2-4 apply to your work situation?

_____

_____

Quality control. The quality of our work is important, but our true worth is not derived from our work.

Read I Corinthians 6:20 — what is the basis of our worth? _____

_____

_____

_____

What does Colossians 3:23-24 say about the quality of our work? _____

_____

_____

From Ephesians 6:6, why would this attitude be effective in a work setting?

_____

_____

_____

II. ACTIONS AS WE WORK

Bloom where you're planted. Paul understood the concept of being an "Insider." As defined by author Jim Petersen, this means God has us right where He wants us. We can serve Him most effectively at the strategic posts in which we find ourselves.

 See Session 2 of *Living Proof II* and Chapter 2 of *Lifestyle Discipleship*, by Jim Petersen, for a deeper understanding of this concept.

Summarize Paul's explanation in 1 Corinthians 7:17 and 24? _____

_____

_____

_____

List three non-believers with whom God has placed you, as an insider, in a work relationship.

_____   _____   _____

Full-time Christian Work? Is it a higher calling to be a pastor/missionary rather than a carpenter or businessman? Explain. _____

_____

_____

_____

It's not a job, it's an adventure! The difficult thing about staying at our posts is that we often find ourselves in antagonistic territory. How do you survive and make a positive impact in a hostile environment? Select below the best description of your work environment:

    a. Believers Inc.
    b. Peaceful Coexistence
    c. Holy War!
    d. Shhh! Don't tell them my secret.
    e. Strugglesville (difficult)
    f. Opportunity Knocking (rewarding)
    g. Other _____

> *"Play the hand God deals, and stop whining."*
> BUMPER STICKER

Describe your personal work (school, etc.) environment. _____

_____

_____

III. EXAMPLE OF DANIEL

Daniel struggled to be true to his faith while held in captivity in Babylon. Read Daniel 5 and 6 for the story. Based on 5:13-14, how does he seem to have lived out his faith?

_____

_____

In 5:22-24, how does Daniel respond in a pressured situation? _____

_____

_____

What does Daniel 6:3,4 reveal about the kind of man Daniel was? _____

_____

Read Daniel 6:6-11. What does this tell us about the visibility of Daniel's character in the face of opposition?

_____

_____

Is Daniel "holier than thou?" Describe his behavior in 6:21-22 (Note that Daniel is in a great position to gloat!). _____

_____

In 6:28, what summary is given for Daniel's experience in a hostile environment?

_____

The Peter Principle. Perhaps it is 1 Peter 2:11-18, which most clearly reveals Daniel's secret. What are some of the temptations (v.11) which most endanger your own witness? _____

_____

What should non-believers see in us? (v.12) _____

_____

Verse 18 refers to slavery, but the principle applies to today's work relationships. In your opinion, how can we follow this difficult command? _____

_____

_____

Environmental Protection. It's logical: if God desires us to hold our posts in enemy territory, He'll stand by us as He did, not only with Daniel, but also with Peter and the early Christians. Employers will mistreat us at times because they are human. Trials will come, but God honors faithfulness.

IV. OVERLOAD

Leaving it Behind. Studies show that Americans are working more hours than ever. There is mounting pressure to achieve. Too often, marriages and families are battle casualties. How much work is too much? God Himself, who needs no rest, established a day of rest at the world's creation. Not only that, He declared that rest holy! (Genesis 2:2-3)

Do you take a day to rest from work? _____ Yes _____ No

List three distractions that keep us from being fruitful as described in Mark 4:18-19.

_____

_____

_____

List distractions in your life with which you struggle. _____

_____

_____

_____

_____

According to Psalm 127:2, what serves as a good indicator that we are working too many hours? _____

_____

Overwork has been shown to be detrimental to physical health. What does work and our body have to do with God, according to 1 Corinthians 3:16-17? _____

_____

_____

_____

_____

"The Bible gives two
fundamental reasons for going to work:
first, God commands it; and second,
it is an environment (but not the only one)
in which the believer can represent Jesus Christ.
The job, then, is a platform for ministry.
The Christian does not work to earn a living.
It is God who provides for his needs."

GORDON ADAMS, VISION FOUNDATION,
WHY GO TO WORK

How do you react to the quote above?_____
_____
_____

How many hours are you spending at work each week? _____

Check yourself by recording the actual number of hours you work this week.

List some attributes and behavior changes that you need to pray about in
regard to your work, school, or homemaking. _____
_____
_____
_____
_____
_____

The Bottom Line. Work is good; it's a precious gift from God. Christians can thrive in the workplace, glorifying God in their pursuit of excellence in attitude and action, as well as in their balance between home, work and other priorities. As we do this, we impact in a powerful way the spiritual climate that moves today's culture; when we don't, the world is a dark place indeed. As we maintain the right perspective and balance we must have clear priorities. These priorities are set by having a clear purpose. We will discuss this in detail in Chapter 5.

Scripture Memory Verse:

2 Work   NIV

COLOSSIANS 3:23
    Whatever you do, work at it with all your heart, as working for the Lord, not for men.

COLOSSIANS 3:23

For additional reading, seminars, resources:

Vision Foundation, Gordon Adams, founder
Books and seminar available:
    Why Go to Work
    Success
Vision Foundation
8901 Strafford Circle
Knoxville, TN 37923
(615) 690-1696

NOTES

_____

_____

_____

_____

_____

_____

_____

_____

_____

_____

_____

_____

_____

_____

_____

_____

_____

_____

_____

_____

_____

_____

_____

_____

_____

_____

_____

3 Handling Money Wisely

Why is there so much month left at the end of the money? ANONYMOUS

There's no reason to be the richest man in the cemetery. You can't do any business from there. COLONEL HARLAN SANDERS

Our pocketbooks have more to do with heaven and also with hell than our hymnbooks. HELMUT THIELICKE

W A R M U P

Many people are uncomfortable when talking about money. What does finance have to do with faith? Plenty, according to Jesus. Sixteen of his thirty-eight parables deal with the handling of money and possessions. About 500 verses in the Bible deal with prayer, less than 500 with faith; yet there are more than 2,000 verses concerning money and possessions. Clearly, there is a Biblical perspective on money and how we use it.

Jump right in. Which of the following best describes your current financial status:

    a. Swimming in money
    b. Head above water
    c. Treading water
    d. Drowning in debt
    e. Other _____

How are you feeling right now about the financial area of your life?

_____

_____

THE BIG PICTURE.

In this chapter, we'll consider five issues:

    I. What is the spiritual nature of money?
    II. What does our handling of money reveal
        about our nature?
   III. How should we view our finances?
   IV. How can we minister through our finances?
    V. How can we put these principles into practice?

I. WHAT IS THE SPIRITUAL NATURE OF MONEY?

Pennies From Heaven. Comment on the source of wealth, according to
I Chronicles 29:11,12. _____

_____

Who is in control? _____

How should this affect our attitude toward money? _____

_____

American currency bears the phrase, "In God we trust." It is a more appropriate
inscription than most people realize.

Is money good? See Ecclesiastes 5:19, and note the attitude we should have.

_____

_____

In Proverbs 3:9, what is a central purpose for the provision given to us? How can we do that?

_____

_____

_____

_____

As we honor God with our money, what trap should be avoided, according to Acts 8:20?

_____

_____

In your opinion, how can we honor God with wealth without trying to "bribe" Him?

_____

_____

There is nothing we handle that reveals the heart inside us like the way we handle money.

II. WHAT DOES OUR HANDLING OF MONEY REVEAL ABOUT OUR NATURE?

In your experience, how have you observed the words of Ecclesiastes 5:10 to be true?

_____

_____

What is the relationship between character and success, according to Proverbs 10:16?

_____

_____

Read carefully I Timothy 6:6-10. Which is evil: money or the love of money? Explain.

_____

According to these verses, what is a positive lifestyle alternative to the love of money?

_____

Why do you think the love of money causes people to wander from their faith?

_____

_____

_____

What light does Matthew 6:24 shed on the previous passage?

_____

_____

Finding freedom. What assurance from Hebrews 13:5 helps us avoid the trap? Explain.

_____

_____

_____

_____

_____

Paul, from a dark, damp prison gives the secret to contentment in Philippians 4:11-13. Explain his point of view. _____

_____

_____

_____

What does Matthew 6:19-21 say about the handling of money and how it relates to our heart? _____

_____

_____

Describe the present relationship between YOUR money and YOUR heart. _____

_____

_____

_____

_____

_____

III. HOW SHOULD WE VIEW OUR FINANCES?

The Ultimate Financial Manager. Could the Bible, a book thousands of years old, offer financial advice relevant to our era? We'll examine some of its prominent teachings.

What basic principle does Jesus establish in Luke 14:28? How does it apply to your finances? _____

_____

_____

What do you discover in Proverbs 13:11? _____

_____

_____

How would you evaluate yourself in light of the wisdom of Proverbs 10:4? *Circle one.*

LAZY　**1**　**2**　**3**　**4**　**5**　**6**　**7**　**8**　**9**　**10**　**DILIGENT**

What surprising secret of success is found in Joshua 1:8? Why do you think it is true?

_____

_____

_____

What is the significance of the phrase "careful to do" in this verse? _____

_____

Digging deeper. The Bible has much more to say about the personal use of money and possessions. We realize that virtually every word of Scriptural truth affects the way we deal with what God has given us. Additional reading, studies and helps are listed at the end of this section.

IV. HOW CAN WE MINISTER THROUGH OUR FINANCES?

In the Parable of the Talents, we discovered that Christ expects us to make the wisest possible use of what has been entrusted to us. Is the goal personal wealth and luxury? Of course not. We're expected to use everything we have to provide for those for whom we are primarily responsible and to serve others as we are able.

How did the first Christians use their resources, according to Acts 4:34-35?

_____

_____

Can you think of a friend who might need your financial help at present?

_____

The early believers supported Christians who travelled to spread the news of Jesus. Summarize Paul's specific instructions in this regard, found in I Corinthians 16:2.

_____

_____

_____

According to II Corinthians 9:23, what is our attitude to be as we give? What attitude are we to avoid? _____

_____

Read Philippians 4:18-19. How does God view such gifts, and what is the result?

_____

_____

How is this principle expressed in Proverbs 11:25? _____

_____

_____

_____

Do you know a Christian worker whom you might support financially and encourage in prayer? (Suggestions: think through who has helped you to grow spiritually, emotionally, etc.? Do they have a need you could meet? Are they in a ministry which is dependent on donations for their support?) _____

_____

_____

_____

As you pray and seek God's guidance, are there changes you might need to make in your use of money? _____

_____

_____

_____

_____

V. HOW CAN WE PUT THESE PRINCIPLES INTO PRACTICE?

To begin to practice these Biblical principles, there are three specific exercises suggested to get you started. If you have already done these sometime in the past, or if you are having difficulty financially, then you may be interested in a group study that would help you work through these issues. Crown Ministries has developed a remarkably effective small group study that trains people to handle money from a biblical perspective. Howard Dayton, the founder, has written a book *Your Money Counts*. You can order this book or find out more about Crown by writing or calling: Crown Ministries, 530 Crown Oak Centre Drive, Longwood, Florida 32750, (407) 331-6000.

1. WHO OWNS IT?

After reflecting on the verses in this lesson, who owns all your possessions, including family, house, money, etc.? _____

Are you willing to make a specific list of all you own and sign this acknowledgement that you are committing it all to God? _____

_____

_____

_____

_____

_____

_____

_____

Signature: _____

2. SIMPLE CASH FLOW: MORE OUTGO, THAN INCOME?

The next step is to determine your cash flow.

The following forms can be copied and used for your personal use. This is the first step in getting control of your finances. Until you see where your finances are currently going, you cannot make a realistic plan or budget.

(These forms are used by permission of Howard Dayton, Crown Ministries and Larry Burkett, Christian Financial Concepts)

FORM 1
THE FAMILY INCOME/EXPENSE WORKSHEET
Monthly Income and Expenses

Income per month $ _____
   Salary   _____
   Other income (Interest, Dividends, Notes, Rents)   _____
   TOTAL GROSS INCOME   _____

Less:
   1. Tithe/Giving   _____
   2. Tax (Federal, State, FICA)   _____

Net Spendable Income:
   3. Housing   _____
        Mortgage (rent)   _____
        Insurance   _____
        Taxes   _____
        Electricity   _____
        Gas   _____
        Water   _____
        Sanitation   _____
        Telephone   _____
        Maintenance   _____
        Other   _____
   4. Food   _____
        Groceries   _____
        Eating Out   _____
   5. Automobiles/Transportation   _____
        Gas and Oil   _____
        Insurance   _____
        License   _____
        Taxes   _____
        Maintenance/Repair/Replacement   _____
   6. Insurance   _____
        Life   _____
        Medical   _____
        Other   _____
   7. Debts (except auto & house payments)   _____
        Credit Card   _____
        Loans & Notes   _____
        Other   _____

8. Entertainment/Recreation _____
    Babysitters _____
    Activities/Trips _____
    Vacation _____
    Pets _____
    Other _____
9. Clothing _____
10. Savings & Investments _____
11. Medical Expenses _____
    Doctor _____
    Dentist _____
    Prescriptions _____
    Other _____
12. Miscellaneous _____
    Toiletry, Cosmetics _____
    Beauty, Barber _____
    Laundry, Cleaning _____
    Allowances, Lunches _____
    Subscriptions _____
    Gifts _____
        Office/Graduation _____
        Birthdays/Anniversary _____
        Weddings/Showers _____
        Christmas _____
    Postage _____
    Accounting/Legal _____
    Financial Services _____
    Special Education _____
    Cash _____
    Other _____
13. School/Child Care _____
    Tuition _____
    Materials _____
    Day Care _____
    Other _____

TOTAL LIVING EXPENSES _____

INCOME VERSUS LIVING EXPENSES

Net Spendable Income   _____

Less Total Living Expenses   _____

Total (Deficit/Surplus)   _____

3. BUDGET: WHERE DOES IT ALL GO?

After working through the previous worksheet, you should be getting some idea where it is all going. The next step is to determine your monthly budget goals. This will be an ongoing exercise because income and expenses are dynamic.

Percentage Guide for Family Income					
GROSS INCOME	20,000	40,000	50,000	60,000	80,000
Tithe/Giving	10%	10%	10%	10%	10%
Taxes	14%	15%	17%	21%	25%
NET SPENDABLE	15,200	30,000	36,500	41,400	52,000
Housing	30%	28%	25%	25%	24%
Auto	15%	12%	12%	12%	11%
Food	16%	14%	14%	10%	9%
Insurance	5%	5%	5%	5%	5%
Entertainment/Rec.	7%	7%	7%	7%	6%
Clothing	5%	5%	6%	6%	6%
Medical/Dental	5%	4%	4%	4%	4%
Miscellaneous	7%	7%	8%	8%	8%
Savings	5%	5%	5%	5%	5%
Debts	5%	5%	5%	5%	5%
Investments/Giving	—	8%	9%	13%	13%

If total expenses are greater than net spendable income, you must cut back on expenses. The percentages for fixed and variable expenses may be adjusted, but your total should add up to 100% and should not exceed your net spendable income.

Use Form 2 to determine a realistic budget for your family. Use the percentage guidelines as they are given in the previous chart for your salary.

Form 2
Budget Percentage Guidelines

Salary for guideline = _____ / year

GROSS INCOME PER MONTH _____

    Tithe (_____% of gross) _____
    Taxes (_____% of gross) _____

NET SPENDABLE INCOME _____

    Housing (_____% of net) _____
    Auto (_____% of net) _____
    Food (_____% of net) _____
    Insurance (_____% of net) _____
    Entertainment/Rec. (_____% of net) _____
    Clothing (_____% of net) _____
    Medical/Dental (_____% of net) _____
    Miscellaneous (_____% of net) _____
    Savings (_____% of net) _____
    Debts (_____% of net) _____
    Investments/Giving (_____% of net) _____

TOTAL *(Cannot exceed net spendable income)* _____

After you have completed these worksheets, look at each category of your actual expenses and your budgeted figures and evaluate how you might decrease or increase the figures to align with the realistic percentages. Set a realistic time frame in which to accomplish your goals, such as paying off all debt, beginning to tithe or opening a savings account, etc.

Suggestion: keep track of your expenses for one month, writing them all down each day.

If you feel completely out of control of your budget, many financial advisers encourage the "envelope" system. Label an envelope for each category and put the set amount of cash in it each payday. When out of cash in that category, stop spending. When all the cash is gone, that's all the spending until the next payday.

If you need more personalized help in this area, talk to your Timothy leader or contact CBMC headquarters, Crown Ministries, or Christian Financial Concepts. Addresses and phone numbers are listed at the end of this lesson.

What has been most helpful to you in this lesson? _____

_____

_____

_____

_____

_____

Scripture Memory Verse:

3 Money   NIV
I CHRONICLES 29:11-12
Yours, O LORD, is the greatness and the power
   and the glory and the majesty and the splendor,
   for everything in heaven and earth is yours.
Yours, O LORD, is the kingdom;
   you are exalted as head over all.
Wealth and honor come from you;
   you are the ruler of all things.
In your hands are strength and power
   to exalt and give strength to all.
                                    I CHRONICLES 29:11-12

You might want to memorize this particular verse in the Living Bible also because it is worded so powerfully.

> Yours is the mighty power and glory and victory and majesty. Everything in the heavens and earth is yours, O Lord, and this is your kingdom. We adore you as being in control of everything. Riches and honor come from you alone, and you are the Ruler of all mankind; your hand controls power and might, and it is at your discretion that men are made great and given strength.
>
> I CHRONICLES 29:11-12, LIVING BIBLE

Opportunity Knocking

The Christian Business Men's Committee organization was raised up by God in the 1930's through the vision of five businessmen. Its purpose is to present Jesus Christ as Savior and Lord to business people and professionals. CBMC develops and produces training resources, such as Operation Timothy studies and Living Proof I and II video series, to equip the body of Christ to evangelize and disciple others. In addition to these training tools, many couples serve CBMC full-time as coaches in various cities in order to encourage and personally meet with Christians who desire to grow spiritually. These couples are supported financially by business and professional people, churches and others who have been helped by their efforts or by using CBMC resources. They live by faith without a set salary. In a true sense, they are missionaries to the business community, depending upon God to meet their needs through those blessed by the ministry. If Operation Timothy has met needs in your life, you might want to pray about financially investing in their lives or in the ministry of developing future training tools. For more information, write or call CBMC headquarters: 1800 McCallie Ave., Chattanooga, TN 37404, 1-800-575-2262.

Additional Resources:
Crown Ministries, Howard Dayton, founder
530 Crown Oak Centre Drive
Longwood, FL 32750 (407) 331-6000
Offers a twelve-week, small group training in finances.
Your Money Counts

Christian Financial Concepts, Larry Burkett, founder
Route 4, Hidden Lake
Dahlonega, GA 30533
Personal Finances
The Financial Planning Workbook
Debt-Free Living, book and cassette and many others

NOTES

4 Moving Toward Maturity

Change — real change — takes place slowly. In first gear, not overdrive. Far too many Christians get discouraged and give up… Breaking habit patterns you established during the passing of years cannot occur in a few brief days. Remember that. Instant change is as rare as it is phony. CHARLES SWINDOLL

We cannot become what we need to be by remaining what we are. MAX DE PREE

Upward bound. With the help of an expert climber, firm rope, and a mountain guide you find yourself high in the sky. You stop to breathe thin air and a sigh of satisfaction. Then you see it: the higher peak, almost hidden by clouds. How can anyone climb it? But your guide says it can be done — but not by amateurs. When we give our lives to Christ, we're offered no ski-lift ride to the top. It's a slow, steady climb, and the greatest thrills are reserved for those who persevere. We need desire, and a more experienced climber to guide us.

As we begin this lesson, how would you grade your own spiritual maturity? Select below the class you would be enrolled in at Discipleship U:
  a. Doctoral program in Spiritual Gianthood
  b. Masters candidate in Advanced Christian Living
  c. Undergraduate degree in Spiritual Survival Training
  d. Remedial Faith 101
  e. Other _____

THE BIG PICTURE.

In this chapter, we'll learn about the process of spiritual maturity, it's components, results and application to me.

I. The process of spiritual maturity.
II. Evangelism as a lifestyle.
III. Discipleship as a lifestyle.
IV. What is the end result?

I. THE PROCESS OF SPIRITUAL MATURITY

As we look at spiritual maturity, we understand that it is a process which consists of a series of events that are tied together. At the heart of this process is a central event — a person receiving Christ as Savior and Lord. We call this "spiritual birth." This central event is the culmination of a process known as evangelism and the springboard for the process known as discipleship. We refer to the overall process as "The Critical Process."

Have you ever experienced "spiritual birth"? _____ If so, from your own life, briefly describe the process that brought you to that point.

_____

_____

Who were the people involved in this process? What was your response to them during this process? _____

_____

_____

A spoon-fed truth. What comparison is given for the maturity process in Hebrews 5:11-13? What are the characteristics of the spiritually mature person? _____

_____

_____

What qualities characterize the mature believer in Philippians 3:12-16? _____

_____

What is the importance of God's Word to this maturing process? Read 1 Peter 2:2.

_____

_____

Examine Philippians 1:6, what is the process described and who is involved in it?

_____

_____

In Galatians 4:19, what was Paul's role in their spiritual maturity process?

_____

Let's summarize with a diagram:

Discipleship as a Lifestyle

Adult

Young Adult

Child

Babe

Birth

Evangelism as a Lifestyle

Harvesting

Sowing

Cultivating

TIME

This is the process of maturing spiritually, known as the "Critical Process." The diagonal line through both boxes above could be called the Critical Path, the path of birth, growth and change that indicates a person who is healthy and is developing more and more Christ-likeness. We will be investigating this process in more depth in the following sections of this lesson. We call it the "critical" process because it is essential, necessary, crucial. If you don't get the overall view of this process and understand its significance for your life, you will be missing out on some of the most exciting parts of this adventure called "The Christian Life!" Note that TIME is a huge factor in this process. Just as it takes years for a baby to grow to adulthood, so it takes a long, long time to grow to spiritual maturity.

Clearly, spiritual maturity doesn't come cheaply or quickly. It carries the price tag of time, dedication, and experience, while continuing to study and apply the Scriptures to your life. But like Jesus' pearl of great price (Matthew 13:45), it's worth giving up everything to attain.

As mentioned in other Timothy lessons, Living Proof I, *Evangelism as a Lifestyle* and Living Proof II, *Discipleship as a Lifestyle,* are two video series that dramatize the process through the lives of several couples. Each series has twelve sessions in which a 15-20 minute video segment is seen, followed by a group discussion. For further information about groups in your area, call CBMC headquarters at 1-800-575-2262.

II. EVANGELISM AS A LIFESTYLE.

Going and Growing. We can't escape the fact that Jesus' last command for us is to help others know Him as we do, and to obey all His teachings. As we are involved in this process, we ask ourselves: do we really know Him? Telling others about Jesus is a lifelong pursuit, but so is the process of getting to know Him better. Spiritual maturity and evangelism are not contradictory, but interdependent. The more we tell others of what we have seen and learned of Christ, the deeper our own hunger grows to know Him even more intimately; and the more intimately we know Him, the more He transforms our lives and the more we want to tell others about Him. We become living proof of what we tell others.

What is the primary point of the parable in Mark 4:3-8?

_____

_____

What metaphor is used? (A metaphor is a comparison)

_____

_____

"The glory of God, and, as our only means to glorifying Him, the salvation of human souls, is the real business of life." C.S. LEWIS

In your own words, how is evangelism like farming? _____

_____

_____

There are three primary stages of farming:

cultivation

sowing

harvesting

Restate Mark 4:20 in your own words, inserting these three stages of farming.

_____

_____

_____

Why is it important to look at evangelism as a process rather than a one-time event?

_____

_____

Lets look at this evangelism/farming part of our diagram:

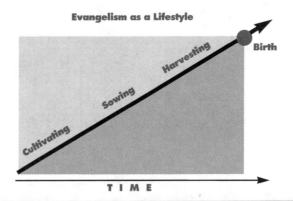

Evangelism as a Lifestyle

Birth

Harvesting

Sowing

Cultivating

T I M E

Chart of the Process of Evangelism

PHASE	I. CULTIVATION	II. SOWING	III. HARVESTING
PICTURE	Soil = Human Hearts	Seed = Gospel Truth	Grain = Reproduced Life of Jesus
EXPLANATION	Speaks to the **heart** through relationship. Focus: caring	Speaks to the **mind** through revelation. Focus: communication	Speaks to the **will** for a faith response. Focus: conversion
EMPHASIS	The **presence** of the believer. Building a friendship bridge.	**Presentation** of the gospel. Giving understanding of truth.	**Persuasion.** Encouraging a meaningful decision of faith.
OBSTACLES	Indifference Antagonism	Ignorance Error	Indecision Love of darkness
SOME EXAMPLES	Nicodemus - John 3 Woman at well - John 4	Ethiopian eunuch - Acts 8 Woman at well - John 4	Jailer - Acts 16 Woman at well - John 4

Have you ever told a friend about Christ who did not accept Jesus Christ as Savior at that time? _____

Was this a failure or was it part of a process? Explain. _____

_____

Below is a chart that is helpful in evaluating where a person might be in this process. Where might the person you shared with (from the previous question) have been in this process? Reflect on the people from your Ten Most Wanted list and other significant people in your life who do not know Christ as Savior and Lord. Where would they be in this process? Where would you place yourself on this chart?

SPIRITUAL AWARENESS CHART

		+6 Reproduction
	Stage IV	+5 Stewardship
	DISCIPLING	+4 Communion with God
SANCTIFICATION	**maturing process**	+3 Conceptual and Behavioral Growth
	(covered in Operation Timothy)	+2 Incorporation into Body
		+1 Post-Decision Evaluation

REGENERATION	**Stage III**	**NEW CREATURE**
C O N V I C T I O N	**HARVESTING picking the crop**	-1 Repentance and Faith
		-2 DECISION to ACT
	Stage II	-3 Personal Problem Recognition
	SOWING	-4 Positive Attitude Toward Gospel
	planting the seed	-5 Grasp of Implications of Gospel
	(i.e. Using Operation Timothy)	-6 Awareness of fundamentals of Gospel
		-7 Positive Attitude Toward the Messenger
	Stage I	-8 Initial Awareness of Gospel
	CULTIVATION	-9 Awareness of Supreme Being but no Knowledge of Gospel
	preparing the soil	-10 No Conscious Awareness of a Supreme Being; may be antagonistic
GENERAL REVELATION		

(right side vertical label: R E J E C T I O N)

GOD'S ROLE	**OUR ROLE**	**MAN'S RESPONSE**

II. DISCIPLESHIP AS A LIFESTYLE.

A disciple is a "person who follows the teachings of another whom he accepts as a leader." Discipleship, when used in a Christian context, means simply "helping another grow spiritually with the goal of Christ being formed in them." (Gal. 4:19)

What metaphor (comparison) is used in I Thessalonians 2:7-11? _____

_____

What roles and attitudes are described in this passage? _____

_____

How does growing spiritually relate to this description of parenting (mothers, fathers, and children)? _____

_____

_____

_____

According to I John 2:11-15, what stages are found in this process of growing up to maturity? What is each stage characterized by? _____

_____

_____

_____

Chuck Swindoll's book, *Growing up in God's Family,* diagrams this process of growing up in the following chart:

The Ages and Stages of Growing Up			
	DESCRIPTION	**STATEMENT**	**FOCUS**
BIRTH/INFANCY	Immaturity	"Help me!"	Surviving
CHILDHOOD	Discovery	"Tell me!"	Learning
ADOLESCENCE	Irresponsibility	"Show me!"	Challenging
ADULTHOOD	Maturity	"Follow me!"	Serving

The "Critical Process" diagram reflects these stages:

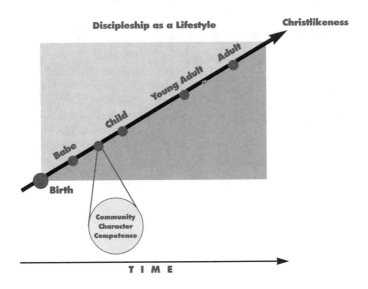

The Three C's. Jim Petersen's book, *Lifestyle Discipleship*, deals with the challenge of spiritual maturity in the modern world. This critical process from baby to adulthood appears to be only one track, but it is actually composed of three tracks, called the 3 "C's": community, competence and character. We can't attain maturity in a vacuum. Other Christians are essential — community. Then we need to learn certain truths, which bring competence as we seek maturity. Finally, perhaps the most important "C" is character. That's who you are when no one's looking. Godly character will not develop without a thorough understanding of God's worldview through studying Scripture.

So it's a challenging mountain ahead. You'll need other climbers for support; you'll need to be competent in climbing skills; and above all, you'll need continually-developing character as you set your gaze upward and begin the climb, one step at a time.

IV. WHAT IS THE END RESULT?

Christ is our goal — to know Him and make Him known. The diagram on page 52 shows clearly that the result of this process called spiritual maturity is increasing Christlikeness. This will have an impact individually as well as on the kingdom of God.

What does God promise as a result in Romans 8:28? To whom is this directed?

_____

_____

I John 3:2. How does John describe the believer at the end of this process?

_____

_____

How does Paul express this spiritual maturity in Colossians 3:4? What do you think this means? _____

_____

_____

What was the joy John described in III John, verse 4? Is this your hope?

_____

_____

The result of this "critical process" will be mature believers who seek to help others grow. This is called spiritual reproduction. How is this detailed when Paul is instructing Timothy in II Timothy 2:2? _____

_____

_____

What kind of man did Paul tell Timothy to invest his life in? _____

_____

How many generations are noted in this verse? _____

Reproduction by multiplication, not addition: One person spends time parenting one other. In two years, each one finds another one, making four. Those four find four others. If each one does this every two years, at the end of twelve years there are 64; at the end of twenty years there are 1,048; at the end of sixty-two years there are 2,176,000,000. Does this concept challenge your thinking? Could you see yourself as an Isaiah 60:22 person?

Have you ever been parented spiritually? By whom? _____

_____

What difference has it made or would it have made if you had had this kind of help early in your Christian life? _____

_____

Are you a part of this kind of reproduction process? _____

What is your desire as you reflect on these issues? _____

_____

What vision does the Lord give to Isaiah in Isaiah 60:22? _____

_____

Where are you in the "critical process?" _____

_____

What indicates this? _____

_____

_____

_____

What new (or renewed) vision and/or insights has God given you as you have
worked through this lesson? _____

_____

_____

_____

_____

_____

Ask God to give you one person, of the same sex, with whom you can put II Timothy 2:2
into action. You can help change the world for Jesus Christ by allowing God to reproduce
His life through you in the life of another. Reflect and continue to pray for those on your
"Ten Most Wanted" list. Then, get ready for the adventure of your life. You are about to
embark on a challenge that has excited men and women for nearly 2000 years — the
opportunity to become directly involved in God's strategy to reach the world.

Scripture
Memory
Verse:

4 Discipleship	NIV

II TIMOTHY 2:2
    And the things you have heard me say in the presence
of many witnesses entrust to reliable men who will also
be qualified to teach others.

II TIMOTHY 2:2

NOTES

5 Multiplying Your Life

LIFE PLAN
GOAL: SLAM DUNK!
STEPS: 1. ____
2. ____
3. ____
4. ____

That's What They Say:

More men fail through lack of purpose than through lack of talent. BILLY SUNDAY

Without a clearly defined purpose, activities will be determined by the pressures and demands of your work, rather than by the Word of God. GORDON ADAMS

WARM UP

Even though most Christians might be clear on what God's overall purpose for their lives is, they often suffer from the same clutter and lack of focus as everyone else.

Spring Cleaning. Your life is like a lived-in home. Take a walk through it, look around, and select the best description of it below:
   a. Not a speck of dust! Clean and uncluttered.
   b. Needs dusting — but it's livable.
   c. Bless this mess!
   d. Other _____

THE BIG PICTURE.

Roll up your sleeves! In this chapter we will accomplish three objectives:

   I. Understanding God's purpose for everyone
   II. Discovering God's unique purpose for me
   III. Assembling a Life Purpose statement

I. UNDERSTANDING GODS PURPOSE FOR EVERYONE

"One size fits all." Who are you? You are a human being with the same biological characteristics as every other member of the species. Then again, you have fingerprints and a genetic blueprint like no other person. In the same way, God gives you a purpose and meaning you share with all other people, but He also has a specific purpose for you. Before anything else, we must understand His purpose for all people as revealed in Scripture.

What is the whole duty of humanity, according to Ecclesiastes 12:13-14?

_____

_____

What purposes for us are revealed in Micah 6:8? _____

_____

_____

How does Jesus define our purpose in terms of two commandments, in Matthew 22:36-40? _____

_____

_____

How are these two commandments related to each other? _____

_____

_____

How did Jesus define His own purpose in Luke 19:10? _____

_____

_____

What becomes of that personal purpose in Matthew 28:19-20? _____

_____

_____

_____

Heir Force. Jesus made us the heirs to purpose. As a matter of fact, as we will see, we are in a real sense His body, living on and working in the world in the same ways He did. We find our purpose as humans as we study His life and values.

We know that the central purpose of Christ is to reach people. Based on Colossians 1:28-29, how are we are to do that and what will our goal be? _____

_____

_____

Based on what we have learned in this section, write a brief Purpose Statement for *all* people. _____

_____

_____

_____

What about me? God's will for all of us is remarkably clear. But what about God's will for one of us? We turn the corner in making that determination when we examine the issue of spiritual gifts, skills, history and other issues.

II. DISCOVERING GOD'S UNIQUE PURPOSE FOR ME

The process of discovering God's own unique purpose for your life cannot be rushed; it is imperative to work at this discovery process over several years, refining and clarifying your purpose as you mature in your faith. Careful investment of your time in thinking through these issues will reward great dividends.

Gordon Adams, in *Establishing Your Purpose,* recommends assessing several areas of life that will help you define and refine your unique purpose:

1. **Spiritual gifts**
2. **Equipping**
3. **Personal skills**
4. **Personal history**
5. **Status**
6. **Temperament**

**Remember:
God's purpose for
all Christians
is to disciple others.
Your spiritual gift will
help you do this.**

1. Spiritual gifts:

What does I Corinthians 10:12 tell us to avoid? Why is this important in the process of discovering God's unique purpose for your life?

_____

_____

Finding your gift. As a Christian, you have at least one spiritual gift. Look at the list in the following chart. Mark a "1" next to the gift that you feel best describes you. Put "2" next to the second best. If you see a third that seems appropriate, mark it also. Next, ask the Christian you most trust and respect to help you evaluate your gifts. A spiritually sensitive person who has observed you in the context of Christian community should be able to help.

Remember, the gifts are not to be used by Lone Ranger Christians! They describe you in terms of function within the body of Christ. Third, pray that the Spirit, who administers the gifts, will make known your special abilities. He will do so clearly as you work, serve and grow in the unity of fellowship.

🗣 SPEAKING GIFTS

Prophecy	Speaks Biblical truth	EPHESIANS 4:11
		ROMANS 12:6
		I COR. 12:28
Teaching	Presents truth practically	EPHESIANS 4:11
		ROMANS 12:6
		I COR. 12:28

🖌 SERVICE GIFTS

Administration	Organizes well; productive	ROMANS 12:28
Helps	Desires to help meet needs	I COR. 12:28
Giving	Gives generously	ROMANS 12:8
Serving	Desires to help others	ROMANS 12:7

🤝 RELATIONAL GIFTS

Encouragement	Builds up; edifies others	ROMANS 12:7
Evangelism	Passion to share the gospel	EPHESIANS 4:18
Hospitality	Warm, inviting, giving nature	ROMANS 12:13
Leadership	Motivates others	ROMANS 12:8
Mercy	Sympathetic, tolerant	ROMANS 12:8
Shepherding	Caring and nurturing	EPHESIANS 4:11

What is the point that I Corinthians 12:14-27 is making in this process of discovering your gifts? _____

_____

_____

2. Equipping:

"Equipping is the process of developing depth in your personal relationship to God through His Word, and breadth in your relationships with other believers and non-believers." (Gordon Adams) The "Hand" illustration describes five ways to assimilate God's Word. Your commitment to master the Bible is essential to being equipped for the purpose God has for you.

Get a grip. Here's a "hands on" approach to living and working with the Word of God.

Do you have a strong grasp on God's Word?

Romans 10:17 — Hear
Revelation 1:3 — Read
Acts 17:11 — Study
Psalm 119:9-11 — Memorize
Psalm 1:2-3 — Meditate

Holy Bible

By permission of The Navigators

The vertical dimension of equipping is our growing depth in the Word, accompanied by a growing, disciplined prayer life. These are the two bases of our communication with God. "The horizontal dimension of equipping is the development of accountability to our brethren and the ability to 'defend the hope that is within you'— evangelism." (Gordon Adams)

What do Hebrews 10:24,25 and 2 Peter 3:15 say about this horizontal dimension?

_____

What are your plans to progress as a person of the Word and prayer?

_____

_____

_____

To whom are you accountable? _____

_____

3. Personal skills:

What you have learned and experienced in life—the areas in which you have developed and demonstrated competence—are your personal skills. These are acquired through effort and discipline.

What are your personal skills? _____

_____

_____

_____

4. Personal history:

"History has to do with your culture, lineage, geography, and general background, all of which affect your lifestyle. Your history or culture has prepared you to serve certain groups or types of people most effectively, and therefore becomes part of your unique purpose. The greatest impact for Christ that a person makes is normally within his or her historical and geographical spheres of influence." (Gordon Adams)

What are several specifics about your culture, lineage, geography, background?

_____

_____

5. Status:

What are the major roles in which you presently find yourself (husband, wife, child, parent, employee or employer, child of God, brother or sister, etc.)?

_____

_____

_____

These roles will largely determine the manifestation of your unique purpose. After reviewing your roles, review God's commands pertaining to each relationship (marriage, Ephesians 5; employee/employer, I Peter 2:18-21, etc.) Unique purpose is to be demonstrated through the application of God's carefully defined commands to each of these relationships.

What are some of God's commands for your roles that indicate your unique purpose?

_____

_____

_____

6. Temperament:

Your personality type will also affect your purpose, for God has endowed you with unique personality traits, and He will use these in your calling. There are several good books and tests that identify different personality types (such as, choleric, sanguine, melancholy, or phlegmatic).

How would you describe your temperament? _____

_____

Getting it together. We've investigated God's purpose for all people and His unique purpose for me. From here, one can begin to formulate a Purpose Statement.

III. ASSEMBLING A LIFE PURPOSE STATEMENT

Life ad lib. In the middle of a battle in *Raiders of the Lost Ark,* Indiana Jones is asked about his plan. "I don't know," he answers, "I'm kind of making it up as I go along." For most people, life is like that: an unpredictable adventure with no set destination or course to get there. From our activities, we conclude what our purpose has been. A wise planner begins with purpose, and moves to activities.

What does Jesus' parable in Matthew 7:24-27 say about the foundation for living?

_____

_____

The future does not
get better by hope,
it gets better by plan.
And to plan for the future
we need goals.

JIM ROHN

Steps toward a Purpose Statement.
First you'll need to do some heavy thinking, praying, and writing.
Use these questions as a worksheet.

1. Start from our common purpose as Christians. Based on our earlier
study, what does God desire from us all? Nothing in the rest of your statement can be
inconsistent with Gods commands, and you won't be successful in other goals if you
ignore His purposes.

2. Who are you? What is your marital status? Family plan? Occupational status?
What special skills are you equipped with? These must all be taken into account.

3. What are your dreams? God gives us special vision and aspiration about
things we desire to happen. When they are in accordance with His laws, they can be
a clue to His will for us.

4. What are your spiritual gifts, skills, temperament, etc?

5. What impressions are you gaining through prayer?
Don't plan without praying.

6. What do godly friends say? Their perspective is essential.

**7. Now take the common purpose and integrate with the other
questions to begin to write a purpose statement.** (Use a legal pad or
notebook to begin your rough draft.)

Name _____

God's universal purpose _____

_____

Your unique gifts, skills, temperament, etc. _____

_____

_____

Career goals _____

_____

_____

Family goals _____

_____

_____

Personal goals _____

_____

_____

What Scripture verses has God used in your life to give you direction and purpose? Choose one of these that best characterizes God's purpose for your life. _____

_____

_____

_____

_____

Be patient: this may take several times of rewriting over a period of time to refine and polish. Discuss this with some close personal friends. Talk to someone who has done this. Ask them to share their purpose statement with you and share how they arrived at it. Sign your name at the bottom of your statement. (If married, this should be done together.)

"A longing fulfilled is sweet to the soul…" Proverbs 13:19

Following are samples of purpose statements from two different couples to give you some idea of how yours might look. Try to write your own in light of the specific gifts and unique calling God has entrusted to you. Remember these were developed over a period of time, re-evaluated periodically, refined, updated. So, just start simply.

If you need more in-depth guidance, Gordon Adams' *Establishing Your Purpose* gives detailed instructions and help in preparing a life purpose statement. Write or call:

Vision Foundation
8901 Strafford Circle
Knoxville, TN 37923
(615) 690-4603

Remember that these are the finished products of a process that took many tries and years to refine. Your first attempt may be a lot simpler than these, but you can continue to work on yours as you grow and learn more. So, don't get discouraged!

Sample 1

LIFE PURPOSE STATEMENT   Date _____

LIFE PURPOSE VERSES

I Thessalonians 2:8

"So being affectionately desirous of you, we were willing to have imparted unto you, not the gospel of God only, but also our own souls, because ye were dear unto us."

II Corinthians 12:15

"And I will very gladly spend and be spent for you; though the more abundantly I love you the less I be loved."

1. To devote my life, to and with my wife (as one), to see that every immediate member of our family becomes a godly Christian. This includes our sons-in-law, their wives (our daughters), grandchildren and grandchildren's children. We will spend time with them as a group and individually in the activities that promote godliness, spending our energy and resources as needed for the accomplishment of this.

2. Our home is given to us by God and shall always be available to Him for everything He wishes to use it for.

3. All our earthly resources belong to God and are available to Him. We are stewards (managers) to utilize these resources as we are directed by God. We will give the tithe regularly as a minimum. The major purpose of the accumulation of our money and resources is to continue our goals after we have gone to Heaven.

4. As much as is possible, we will direct our everyday work and play activities toward the CBMC purpose which we have been called to, and which we feel is synonymous with the Great Commission. Matthew 28: 19, 20.

5. We will seize every opportunity presented to us to share Jesus Christ as the only Savior and Lord and answer for the sin of individual man. We depend upon the Holy Spirit for our direction in these matters as we understand that this battle for people's souls is supernatural.

6. We are committed to the training of a few people personally as disciplemakers and leaders. Understanding that this takes a tremendous amount of energy and time, we plan 2-8 years with individual people that God entrusts to us.

7. We remain open to the Lord for every new learning experience. We desire to grow spiritually and realize that God keeps us in a training program. It is our desire to be in this learning program until we are promoted to Heaven and our eternal promises.

8. We are learning to establish goals for each category stated and want the Lord to hold us accountable for setting and maintaining this LIFE PURPOSE statement. Each of these statements should be broken into segments reflecting both short-range and long-range goals. These should be checked monthly, noted for progress quarterly and updated for accuracy and accomplishment yearly. We will schedule regular time on a calendar for planning and prayer.

Sample 2

LIFE PURPOSE STATEMENT   Date _____

My Purpose: "Love the Lord my God with all my heart and with all my soul and with all my mind…Love my neighbor as myself." Matthew 22:37-38

1. Love the Lord my God
  with all my heart
  with all my soul
  with all my mind.

  a. Make time daily getting to know and love God more intimately, through reading the Bible, prayer, memorizing, meditating and applying Scripture to every area of my life (spiritual, emotional, physical, spouse, children, work, leisure, friends, family, etc.)

  b. Spend time daily with my wife and children getting to know God through family devotions, attending family conferences, Bible studies. Take each child through Operation Timothy when he/she is old enough and spiritually ready to receive it.

  c. Worship and study with other believers at least weekly.

  d. Ongoing, personal Bible study that deepens my understanding of and love for God in Scripture.

2. Love my neighbor as myself.

  a. Take care of myself as a cherished, valuable creation of God Himself. This includes balance of physical exercise and nutrition, spiritual growth, emotional outlets of play, meaningful friendships and relationships, rest, work. I know that I depend upon God to fill up my tank in these areas so that I might give to others from a full, not empty, tank.

  b. Love the "neighbors" God has put in my life: my spouse first, my children, my extended family, friends, neighbors, co-workers, and others. This includes spending quality and quantity time with each of them in getting to know each other, playing together, sharing Christ, meeting each other's needs, worshipping together.

  c. Ask God to give me one person, of the same sex, that I can spiritually parent through Operation Timothy. Meet with him/her regularly in Bible study, and frequently for fun activities.

  d. Give to my local church, missionaries, Christian organizations as the Lord leads me.

GOALS TO FACILITATE A LIFE PURPOSE STATEMENT
EXAMPLES

	Goals	Purpose	Verse
FAMILY	1. Read God's Word together daily and memorize Scripture 2. Spend time with spouse and children daily — education and sports 3. Eliminate television — promote reading and play.	To strengthen family bonds and put God's words in our heart. To educate our children in the ways of the Lord.	Deuteronomy 6:6,7
SPIRITUAL	1. To read through Bible in a year, using Daily Walk Bible 2. Increase our prayer time — maintain a prayer journal	To know God better, to understand His will for our lives, and to have a more abundant life.	John 17:3
FINANCIAL	1. To live within our budget 2. To get out of all debt	To keep from increasing our debt and to begin laying aside the financial weights that hinder our life purpose.	Proverbs 22:7
PHYSICAL	1. Ride the bike every weekday early in the morning	To maintain our health, lean bodies, and to be more joyful and appealing witnesses.	Hebrews 12:11
SOCIAL	1. To stay active with Christian and non-Christian couples and friends 2. To be on time all of the time	To be effective salt and light, to reach others for Christ.	Matthew 5:13

How would having a written purpose statement help you fulfill God's original command of "Be fruitful and multiply"? _____

_____

_____

Read Isaiah 60:22. Replace "the least of you" with your name. What is your reaction?

_____

_____

_____

Do you believe God would want to multiply you spiritually?

_____

_____

Scripture Memory Verse:

5 Spiritual Multiplication   NIV

ISAIAH 60:22
> The least of you will become a thousand,
>   the smallest a mighty nation.
> I am the LORD;
>   in its time I will do this swiftly.

ISAIAH 60:22

Reference:
Establishing Your Purpose, Gordon Adams

NOTES

6 Seeing the World God's Way

That's What They Say:

> *Flying at 600 feet elevation, an eagle can spot an object the size of a dime moving through six-inch grass. The same creature can see three-inch fish jumping in a lake five miles away. Eaglelike people can envision what most would miss. Visionary people see beyond the hum-drum of everyday activities into future possibilities.*
> CHARLES SWINDOLL, *COME BEFORE WINTER*

> *Jesus did not pray that His disciples should be taken out of the world. He never prayed that they might find escape; he prayed that they might find victory.* WILLIAM BARCLAY

W A R M   U P

Ready for the World. The thoughts of Paul, the apostle, turned frequently to his younger friend Timothy. Like a father, he had seen the younger man through spiritual childhood and adolescence. The time finally came when Timothy had put away the childish things and stood ready to face the world. Paul helped Timothy to understand that the ultimate task of every Christian is to begin to see the world as God sees it.

> "I have no one else like him (Timothy), who takes a genuine interest in your welfare. For everyone looks out for his own interests, not those of Jesus Christ. But you know that Timothy has proved himself, because as a son with his father he has served with me in the work of the gospel."
>
> **PHILIPPIANS 2:20-22**

THE BIG PICTURE.

In this lesson, we will learn

I. **How to do the Advanced ABC Bible Study**
II. **How Jesus views the world from John 17**
III. **Seeing the world God's way**

I. HOW TO DO THE ADVANCED ABC BIBLE STUDY

Our two-fold objective for this chapter is to see the world God's way as we learn a Bible study method known as the Advanced ABC. We will investigate John 17.

"Question-and-answer Bible studies are the most popular approach to studying the Scriptures…[they] serve especially well as an introduction to the Scriptures for new and growing Christians…By touching on a variety of topics throughout the Bible in a relatively short time, these studies can build a foundation for understanding major scriptural teachings." However, it is invaluable to any growing disciple to learn how to study the Scriptures on his own. An inductive, analytical approach enables every student of the Word to gain a deeper understanding of a passage.

The Navigator Bible Studies Handbook is a comprehensive look at the different types of Bible study with samples and reproducible forms. It covers how to do verse, chapter and book analyses, as well as topical and Bible character studies. Operation Timothy is a question-and-answer, topical Bible study. This lesson will introduce you to one of the methods from the Handbook, called the Advanced ABC Bible Study that will enable you to continue to study the Bible on your own.

The Navigator Bible Studies Handbook (p.54-68), with permission from The Navigators and NavPress: to order or for more information, call CBMC, 1-800-575-2262 or NavPress, 1-719-548-9222.

Room with a View. On his last evening with the disciples, Jesus gathered them into a private room and poured out His heart to them. John Chapters 13-17 covers his entire discourse. Chapter 17, in particular, has come to be known as the "high priestly prayer." Though facing His own death, His vision and heart was for others.

We will see Jesus' heart and vision as we learn how to study this wonderful passage of Scripture. You should read through the chapter slowly and prayerfully at least once as you start your study, then once aloud, and once pausing at the end of each verse to reflect on what you have read. (You may want to write down the number of times you have read the chapter in each of these ways.) Using your own Bible, or the passage printed in the text, do the reading as suggested above. As you read, you might use different colored pencils or various symbols to mark repeated words, lists, contrasts, comparisons, the use of God, Jesus, or Spirit. For instance, you might draw a cross every time the word "Jesus" or a pronoun for Jesus is used, as demonstrated for you in John 17 on pages 86 and 87. The word "world" is repeated often in John 17. Underline or mark "world" and other repeated words. This will help you observe the text carefully. You might want to make a copy of John 17 to work on while you do this study.

When you have read through the chapter and observed it carefully, then begin filling in the ABC Bible Study form below.

THE ADVANCED ABC BIBLE STUDY

Date: _____

Study Passage: John 17

Times Read:

Slowly: _____ Aloud:_____ In verse-by-verse meditation:_____

Other times: _____ Time spent on study:_____

The Advanced ABC Bible Study has seven parts:

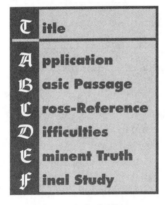

𝕿 itle

𝕬 pplication

𝕭 asic Passage

𝕮 ross-Reference

𝕯 ifficulties

𝕰 minent Truth

𝕱 inal Study

We will explain each of these with some helpful hints as we go along. We have provided a few examples for each section to stimulate your thinking. There aren't right and wrong answers to these studies, such as, one basic passage. If three people did the basic passage they might come up with three different references. Sometimes it will be the same. It is important to explain why you saw that particular reference as basic to the passage.

You can do your Title, Eminent Truth and Application more effectively after combing through the chapter verse by verse on some of the other sections. Try to budget a certain amount of time for each section to ensure spending some time on each part of the study. Keep a record of time spent and record it on your form. (A blank, reproducible form is included at the end of this lesson for future studies).

As you are working on one section of your study, a good verse or idea might come to you regarding another section. Write it down on a separate sheet of paper and go back to the section you are working on. It is probably better to do the study in rough draft form first, then transfer it neatly to the final form.

Basic Passage:
In this section, select one (and no more than three) verse(s) which contain the dominant theme — basic truth — of John 17. After reading through the chapter, start with verse one and consider whether it might be the basic passage. Continue through the chapter looking at each verse in this way. You may end up with several possible basic passages; eliminate all but your final choice. Write the reference and the verse(s) out in the space provided for the Basic Passage below.

BASIC PASSAGE

Example 1: verse 3,   *"Now this is life eternal, that they may know you; the only true*

God and Jesus Christ whom you have sent."

Example 2: verses 17-18,   *"Sanctify them by the truth; your word is truth. As you sent me*

into the world, I have sent them into the world."

Your ideas:

_____

_____

_____

Your final choice:

_____

_____

Cross-References:
Because the complete teaching on any subject is not found in just one chapter, it is good to compare Scripture with Scripture. The best commentary on the Bible is the Bible itself. Consider each verse or passage carefully, meditate on it, then try to remember good cross-references for that particular section. You may also use a concordance or marginal references in your Bible. Choose cross-references that support the thought by adding information, giving an example, or revealing a different viewpoint. You don't have to cross-reference every verse, but it may be helpful to increase your understanding of the chapter.

CROSS-REFERENCE

Under the columns titled VERSE, CROSS-REFERENCE, and KEY THOUGHT, write the number of the verse in John 17 to which the cross-reference relates, then the cross-reference, and two or three words giving the central truth which links the two verses. Several examples are provided for you.

Verse	Reference	Key Thought
v.3	*I John 5:11-13*	*Eternal life = Christ indwelling us*
v.9	*Romans 8:26*	*Holy Spirit intercedes for us*
v.20	*Hebrews 7:25*	*Christ lives to intercede for us*
v.26	*John 3:16,17*	*God sent His Son to die for me*

Verse	Reference	Key Thought

CROSS-REFERENCE

Difficulties:

Difficulties: Questions will arise as you read through John 17. Asking the question "Could I explain this verse to someone else?" will help you to identify those questions, problems, or difficulties. Write down the verse number and the particular question, not just "I don't understand." When you have completed your other study sections, you may want to come back to this one and see if any of the difficulties were resolved through your study, or you may want to do some additional research. When you find an answer, write it down.

DIFFICULTIES

Example 1: *"None has been lost except the son of perdition." Does this contradict the verse elsewhere that says "God: who will have all men to be saved."?*

Example 2: *Is Christ still praying for me now? What does it mean to "keep them from the evil one."*

Final Study: Even though this section is entitled FINAL STUDY, it may be more helpful to work on this section at this point. This part focuses on observation of the text: "What does it say?" rather than "What does it mean?" Accurately explaining the meaning or interpreting Scripture depends greatly on careful and precise observation first. You will either summarize or outline John 17 at this point. This will enable you to put the actual content of the chapter into your own words.

For a *summary,* write a brief synopsis of John 17. Be sure to include all parts of the chapter, not giving too much space to one part and neglecting another. Write one sentence for each successive thought in the chapter, using your own words. Then, condense your summary into fewer words, combining your sentences and restating more briefly. Try to aim for an average of 2 -8 words per verse.

If you choose to do an *outline* instead of a summary, divide John 17 into its natural sections or paragraphs, giving a brief title or heading for each in your own words. Beside the title, note the verses for that section. Then under each of the main headings list as many subpoints as you need to indicate the contents briefly. An outline might look like this:

    I.   Main Heading or Title for this Division (17:1-6)
         A.   Subpoint (verses 1-3)
         B.   Subpoint (4-6)

    II.   Main Heading (17:7-19)
         A.   Subpoint (7-12)
             1.   Subpoint (7-9)
             2.   Subpoint (10-12)
         B.   Subpoint (13-19)
             1.   Subpoint (13-15)
             2.   Subpoint (16-19)

    III.   Main Heading (20-26)
         A.   Subpoint (20-23)
         B.   Subpoint (24-26)

FINAL STUDY

Summary or Outline

Here is a sample outline for John 17. Several of the headings have been filled in for you, with

blanks at several places for you to fill in your summary of what those verses say. You may also

want to come up with your own outline or summary. This one is just to give you some ideas.

I. Personal Prayer to His Father v. 1-5

  A. The Father and Son be glorified, v.1

  B. Eternal life to all whom God gave, v.2-3

II. Prayer for Christ's Disciples, v.6-19

  A. They would remain faithful (kept in Thy name), v.6-12

  B. v.13:

  C. v.14-16:

  D. v.17-18:

  E. v.18-19:

III. Prayer for Oneness, v.20-26

  A. Oneness, v.21-23

    1. Unity with one another

    2. Intimacy with God and Christ

  B. Be a witness to the world

  C. v.24:

  D. v.25-26:

Title: Next, title John 17 in your own words. On a separate sheet of paper write down two or three titles that come to your mind as you study; then either select the best one or combine them. The title should fit the chapter and be as complete as possible. Clearly identify the chapter content and don't worry about making the title catchy. It can be from one to eleven words long. Some people find this easier to do near the end of the study, others at the beginning.

TITLE

Sample Titles: Jesus' World Report to the Father.   Jesus' Final Prayer.

    God's Heart Revealed through Christ's Prayer.

Your Title:

Eminent Truth: This is the main teaching of John 17, but may center in a small portion or a single verse. It is a "miniature topical or doctrinal" study within the chapter. Your basic passage will often be the basis of the eminent truth.

Ask yourself, "Is this the *main* truth or spiritual principle the Holy Spirit is teaching in this chapter?" First state the truth, in your own words, then develop it with various points from the rest of the chapter. As much as possible, document your statements with specific verses from within the chapter. You may also use your cross-references.

Example 1:

What is on the heart of God (Jesus Christ) is people. [Forty-two times personal pronouns are used, particularly "you"]. Just as God sent Christ into the world to reconcile man to God, Christ sent the apostles (and those who would believe in the future) into the world with His message. Christ prays for all His disciples (and all future believers) that they would experience the same oneness with God that He had, unity with one another, and, as a result, the world would believe in Him. Because this prayer is Christ's last large set of words before the cross, it is of utmost significance.

Example 2:

From basic passage verses 2,3: Because of the authority over all people given the Lord Jesus Christ by God, the Father, Jesus completed what He came to do in three years. Jesus now prays for those God has given Him and their future. God's heart is for His disciples and those who will believe in Him. Christ's words on the cross "It is finished" is a confirmation of this prayer. This prayer reveals the kind of intimate relationship that the Father and Son had, which Christ wanted for all His disciples to experience with God and with each other.

EMINENT TRUTH

Application: Usually, you will want to do this section near the end of your study. You may have guessed already that the order of the sections is not the order in which you may necessarily work on them. They are in that order to correspond to the acrostic A,B,C,D,E,F.

Your application will spell out some practical way you can glorify God by obeying His Word. It may speak of something God wants you to do or stop doing, some habit you need to form or break, or imply a new awareness of some truth to incorporate into your thinking. Often, you may become aware of some ways God has already begun applying these truths in your life and has now given you a new understanding of Him and His ways. Choose your application either in relation to God or in relation to others. In relation to God, your application may be an appreciation of some great truth which deepens your devotion to Him, leads to some needed correction in attitude, or strengthens or improves your fellowship with Him. It may also involve some promise or command that affects your relationship with Him. If your application is in relation to others, it will aim toward improving your relationship with fellow Christians or with those who do not know Jesus Christ. This type of application usually relates to your outreach and service for the Lord.

Jesus instructed his disciples: "Now that you know these things, you will be blessed if you do them" (John 13:17)

Begin by writing the number of the verse(s) from which you are taking your application. Then state in your own words the truth of the verse(s). Use personal pronouns: "I," "me," "my," and "mine." Tell what the truth reveals in your life, what shortcomings, transgressions, or neglect it indicates, or what new appreciation or understanding it opens up for you. If possible, mention an incident in your life which illustrates the failure or need.

Transformation comes through renewing our minds rather than being conformed to the pattern of this world. (Romans 12:1,2)

Then state clearly what you plan to do about this through God's grace and power. Tell what specific action you will take to correct this weakness, to build the needed quality into your life, or to increase your understanding of this truth. Be realistic. Choose something practical that you can do within the following week, instead of a long-term project. Your next Bible study will bring a new application to work on.

Practical suggestions for applications:
- writing a letter
- memorizing a verse
- praying about a special need
- doing a kindness
- making an apology and asking forgiveness
- taking a step toward forming or breaking a habit.

You should also have a checkup plan to remind you to carry out your application. And remember that for every step of growth in your Christian life, you must depend on the Holy Spirit.

Two Sample Applications:

Example 1: Refocus my prayer life for those I am spiritually parenting, and for those "Timothies" they will someday parent, praying for our single purpose to be a witness to the world of Christ's love.

Example 2: Daily read through John 17 this week,

> *a) meditating on the key words "you" (39 times), "to the Father", and "world" (17 times), and*

> *b) praising God for His perfect plan for our salvation and eternal life.*

> *Review my life purpose statement and update it from the things I have learned in John 17.*

[*The Navigator Bible Studies Handbook* also has sample chapter studies that illustrate this process in more detail, if you need additional help in completing this lesson.]

II. HOW DOES JESUS VIEW THE WORLD?

Jesus prays, in John 17:11, for divine protection for us. For what purpose does He say He is protecting us? _____

_____

Why is this important? _____

_____

What is Jesus' solution for the challenges Christians face in John 17:15? _____

_____

_____

What are some ways discouraged Christians might be tempted to bail "out of this world?" _____

_____

_____

Give a brief explanation, in your own words, of the common phrase: "in the world but not of it." _____

_____

To whom does Jesus enlarge the boundaries of His prayer in John 17:20? _____

_____

What do we begin to understand about Jesus' world view as we reach verse 20? _____

_____

_____

What does the unity of the Son and the Father have to do with our unity? (v.21) _____

_____

_____

III. SEEING THE WORLD GOD'S WAY

Fill in the blanks to show who Jesus prays for in John 17:

First, He prays for _____ (v.1).

Next, He prays for _____ (v.9).

Finally, He prays for _____ (v.20).

Why is this particular order important? _____

_____

 In what ways has studying John 17 helped you "to see the world God's way?"

_____

_____

_____

_____

Scripture Memory Verse:

6 Great Commission   NIV

MATTHEW 28:19-20
  Therefore go and make disciples of all nations, baptizing them in the name of the Father and of the Son and of the Holy Spirit, [20] and teaching them to obey everything I have commanded you. And surely I am with you always, to the very end of the age.

MATTHEW 28:19-20

Challenge: Memorize several verses from John 17.

THE ADVANCED ABC BIBLE STUDY

Date: _____

Study Passage: _____

Times Read:

Slowly: _____ Aloud:_____ In verse-by-verse meditation:_____

Other times: _____ Time spent on study:_____

Title: _____

$\mathcal{A}$pplication:

_____
_____
_____
_____
_____
_____
_____
_____

$\mathcal{B}$asic Passage:

_____
_____
_____
_____
_____
_____
_____
_____
_____
_____
_____
_____

Cross-Reference:

Verse: **Reference:**   **Key Thought:**

_____

_____

_____

_____

_____

_____

_____

_____

_____

_____

Difficulties:

Verse: **Question:**

_____

_____

_____

_____

_____

Eminent Truth:

_____

_____

_____

_____

_____

Final Study:

JOHN 17

¹After Jesus said this, he looked toward heaven and prayed: "Father, the time has come. Glorify your Son, that your Son may glorify you. ²For you granted him authority over all people that he might give eternal life to all those you have given him. ³Now this is eternal life: that they may know you, the only true God, and Jesus Christ, whom you have sent. ⁴I have brought you glory on earth by completing the work you gave me to do. ⁵And now, Father, glorify me in your presence with the glory I had with you before the world began.

⁶"I have revealed you to those whom you gave me out of the world. They were yours; you gave them to me and they have obeyed your word. ⁷Now they know that everything you have given me comes from you. ⁸For I gave them the words you gave me and they accepted them. They knew with certainty that I came from you, and they believed that you sent me. ⁹I pray for them. I am not praying for the world, but for those you have given me, for they are yours. ¹⁰All I have is yours, and all you have is mine. And glory has come to me through them. ¹¹I will remain in the world no longer, but they are still in the world, and I am coming to you. Holy Father, protect them by the power of your name — the name you gave me — so that they may be one as we are one. ¹²While I was with them, I protected them and kept them safe by that name you gave me. None has been lost except the one doomed to destruction so that Scripture would be fulfilled.

¹³"I am coming to you now, but I say these things while I am still in the world, so that they may have the full measure of my joy within them. ¹⁴I have given them your word and the world has hated them, for they are not of the world any more than I am of the world. ¹⁵My prayer is not that you take them out of the world but that you protect them from the evil one. ¹⁶They are not of the world, even as I am not of it. ¹⁷Sanctify them by the truth; your word is truth. ¹⁸As you sent me into the world, I have sent them into the world. ¹⁹For them I sanctify myself, that they too may be truly sanctified.

²⁰"My prayer is not for them alone. I pray also for those who will believe in me through their message, ²¹that all of them may be one, Father, just as you are in me and I am in you. May they also be in us so that the world may believe that you have sent me. ²²I have given them the glory that you gave me, that they may be one as we are one: ²³I in them and you in me. May they be brought to complete unity to let the world know that you sent me and have loved them even as you have loved me.

²⁴"Father, I want those you have given me to be with me where I am, and to see my glory, the glory you have given me because you loved me before the creation of the world.

²⁵"Righteous Father, though the world does not know you, I know you, and they know that you have sent me. ²⁶I have made you known to them, and will continue to make you known in order that the love you have for me may be in them and that I myself may be in them."

NOTES

lined note paper with no written content

CONCLUSIONS AND RECOMMENDATIONS

Congratulations! This part of your journey in getting to know God more intimately is finished, but this is only the beginning! Following are a few suggestions on the next steps you might take to continue growing toward Christlikeness:

1. Study the OT Leader's Guide:
   Take several weeks to go through the Operation Timothy Leader's Guide with your leader. Begin praying about going through OT with another person or couple.

2. Find your own Timothy:
   Look for people who have the following characteristics:
   a. Heart for God
   b. Teachability
   c. Faithfulness
   d. Willingness to teach others
   Make a list of people who have these qualities or the potential to develop them and pray for them. Your "Timothy" may be a person you have had the privilege of leading to Christ, or a young, immature Christian, or even a non-Christian who is willing to explore God's Word, perhaps someone on your "Ten Most Wanted" List.

3. Continue to dig deep into God's Word.
   One idea is to do an Advanced ABC Bible study on the book of I Thessalonians. Also, continue to memorize and meditate on Scripture (you may want to do the Navigators' Topical Memory System).

4. Read Jim Petersen's books, *Living Proof,* and *Lifestyle Discipleship,* and Dr. Richard Swenson's book, *Margin.*

5. Participate in Living Proof I and II group studies.

6. Participate in a Crown Ministry group study.

7. Begin attending CBMC Family Conferences with your family. Invite other couples to go with you. Other seminars and training opportunities will greatly enhance and encourage your growth in the Lord.

ACKNOWLEDGEMENTS

So many people have contributed to the process of revising Operation Timothy that it would be impossible to name them all. However, we would like to thank all who have given their time and energy to this project. To you God says, "Well done, thou good and faithful servant."

Special thanks belong to the following:
- The original Operation Timothy Task Force (first meeting, June 3-5, 1992: Joe and Gladys Coggeshall, Gordon Adams, Mike and Carol Marker, Jim and MaryGail Lyon, Jim and Betty Orders, Karen Mitchell, Dave Stoddard, Pete George, Bob Tamasy, Bernie Ritterbush, Ralph Hunt)

- Team Resources (Pat MacMillan, David Schmidt)

- The Livingstone Corporation (James Galvin, Dave Veerman)

- John Baggenstoss, Ebsco Media

- Pastors: Andy Stanley, Dave Pridemore, Jay Street

- CBMC staff and members (Phil Downer, Craig Kiggens, Fred Zillich, Dave Rathkamp, Clif Campbell, Kevin Ring, Fritz Klumpp)

- All those CBMCers and others who gave valuable feedback and generous gifts to fund this project

- Operation Timothy Development Team: Joe Coggeshall, Bruce Witt, Donna Williams

- Proofreaders: Dana Witt, Deborah Dickerson

Extraspecial thanks to Isa Williams, graphic designer, for your commitment to excellence in designing and integrating the concept, graphics, covers, and overall format. To Rob Suggs, writer and cartoonist, thank you for all the patience and creativity you brought to our ideas and content.

Make A Real Difference!

One of the ways that you could help us tremendously is to return the following evaluation. It only takes a few minutes and will give us the feedback we need to continue developing resources for the body of Christ. Just cut or tear out this sheet, fax to (423) 629-4434 or fold and mail to the address printed on the back. To order more Operation Timothy sets or Living Proof Video I and II, call the toll-free number listed below.

Date _____

Name _____

Address _____

Telephone (B) _____ (H) _____

(Fax) _____

I have completed this Operation Timothy series:

   Book 1   Book 2   Book 3   Book 4

I am currently going through OT as: a leader   a learner

I used the Leader's Guide in preparation for the sessions: Yes   No

On scale of 1 (low) to 5 (high), evaluate the following issues:

   Will continue to use OT in discipling others   1 2 3 4 5

   OT is user friendly   1 2 3 4 5

   Gives Christians and new Christians a healthy start   1 2 3 4 5

   Is being used in my church   1 2 3 4 5

Church name, pastor, address _____

_____

_____

I've completed Living Proof I: Evangelism as a Lifestyle   Yes   No

   Living Proof II: Discipleship as a Lifestyle   Yes   No

   Crown Ministry 12-week study   Yes   No

Comments: _____

_____

_____

For more information or to order,
call 1-800-575-2262

CBMC of USA
1800 McCallie Ave.
Chattanooga, TN 37404